![Collins]

Easy Learning

Handwriting Workbook 2

Age 5-7

Karina Law

This book belongs to

How to use this book

- Easy Learning workbooks help your child improve basic skills, build confidence and develop a love of learning.

- Find a quiet, comfortable place to work, away from distractions.

- Get into a routine of completing one or two workbook pages with your child every day.

- Ask your child to circle the star that matches how many activities they have completed every two pages:

Some = half of the activities   Most = more than half   All = all the activities

- The progress certificate at the back of this book will help you and your child keep track of how many ⭐ have been circled.

- Encourage your child to work through all of the activities eventually, and praise them for completing the progress certificate.

- Each workbook builds on the previous one in the series. Help your child complete this one to ensure they have covered what they need to know before starting the next workbook.

- Help your child to rest their pencil in the 'V' between their thumb and index finger; their fingers should be between one and two centimetres away from the pencil tip.

- Introduce your child to the 'starting point' in each activity, where they should first place their pencil or pen on the paper.

- You may find that it helps your child to say aloud the patterns and words as they write.

Parent tip
Look out for tips on how to help your child with handwriting practice.

- Ask your child to find and colour the little monkeys that are hidden throughout this book.

- This will help engage them with the pages of the book and get them interested in the activities.

(Don't count this one.)

Published by Collins
An imprint of HarperCollins*Publishers*
77–85 Fulham Palace Road
Hammersmith
London
W6 8JB

Browse the complete Collins catalogue at
www.collinseducation.com

First published in 2011
© HarperCollins*Publishers* 2011

10 9 8 7 6 5 4

ISBN 978-0-00-727757-5

The author asserts the moral right to be identified as the author of this work.

British Library Cataloguing in Publication Data
A catalogue record for this publication is available from the British Library

Written by Karina Law
Based on content by Sue Peet
Design and layout by Linda Miles, Lodestone Publishing
Illustrated by Graham Smith, Andy Tudor and Jenny Tulip
Cover design by Linda Miles
Cover illustration by Jenny Tulip and Kathy Baxendale
Packaged and project managed by White-Thomson Publishing Ltd
Printed and bound by Printing Express, Hong Kong

Contents

How to use this book   2

Count to ten   4

Patterns: Fireworks!   5

Letter shapes: l, t, i   6

Letter shapes: u, j, y   7

Letter shapes: r, n, h, b   8

Letter shapes: m, k, p   9

Letter shapes: c, a, o   10

Letter shapes: d, e, g   11

Letter shapes: q, f, s   12

Letter shapes: v, w, x, z   13

Rhyming words   14

Word endings: ff, ll, ss   15

Word endings: ck   16

Word endings: ng   17

Vowel sounds: ai, ay   18

Days of the week   19

Vowel sounds: ee, ea   20

Vowel sounds: ie, igh, y   22

Vowel sounds: oa, ow   24

Vowel sounds: oo   26

Question words   27

Jokes   28

Handwriting practice: 'I've got a dog…'   29

Capital letters   30

You've got mail!   31

Count to ten

Trace the numbers, then write them out. Start at the green dot.

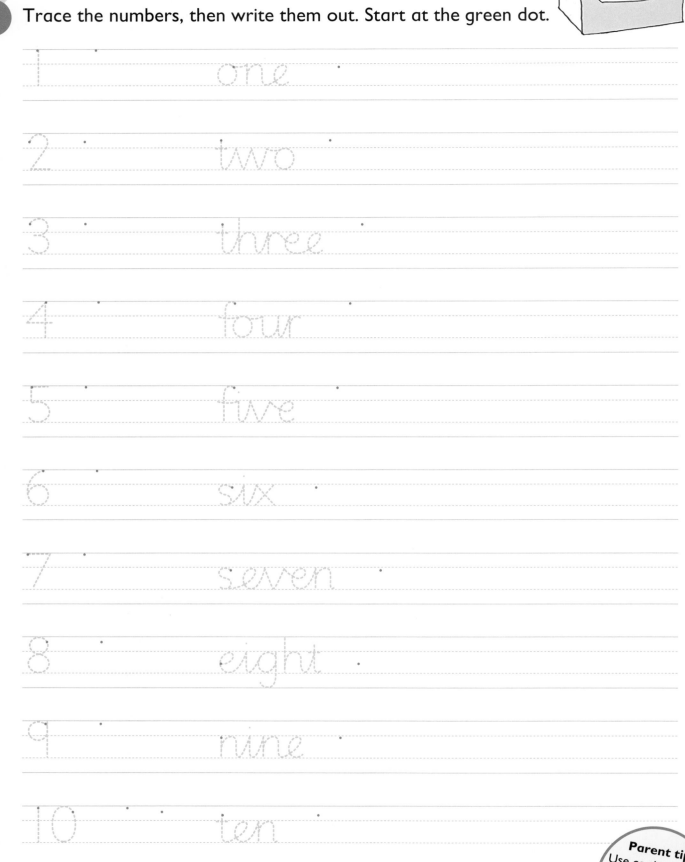

1   one

2   two

3   three

4   four

5   five

6   six

7   seven

8   eight

9   nine

10   ten

Parent tip
Use cookie dough to make number- and letter-shaped biscuits.

Patterns: Fireworks!

2 Follow the arrows and draw over the broken lines to complete the firework patterns. Start at the green dot.

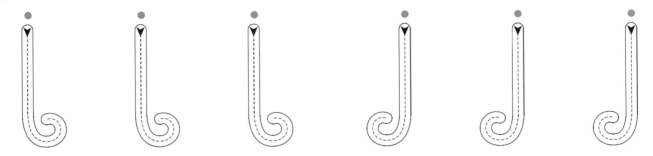

3 Follow the arrows and draw over the broken lines to complete the firework patterns. Start at the green dot.

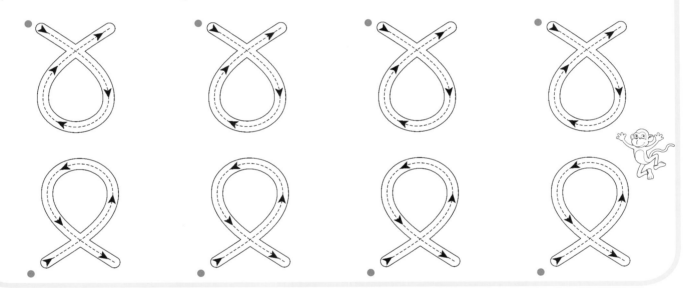

4 Follow the arrows and draw over the broken lines to complete the firework patterns. Start at the green dot.

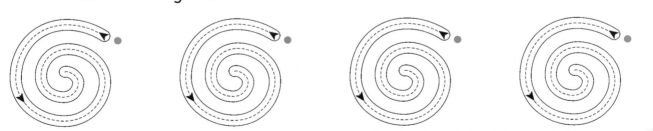

How much did you do?   Activities 1–4

Circle the star to show what you have done.

 Some

 Most

 All

Letter shapes: l, t, i

1 Trace and write. Start at the green dot.

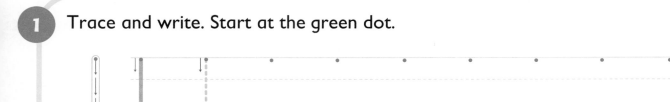

l l l l

lamp leg lion

2 Trace and write. Start at the green dot.

t t t t

tin taxi tent

3 Trace and write. Start at the green dot.

i i i i

ink ill insect

4 Read and write.

Little lions licking their lips.

Letter shapes: u, j, y

5 Trace and write. Start at the green dot.

up   ugly   under

6 Trace and write. Start at the green dot.

jam   jelly   jump

7 Trace and write. Start at the green dot.

yes   yo-yo   yawn

8 Read and write.

Ugly bugs under an umbrella.

How much did you do?   Activities 1–8

Circle the star
to show what
you have done.

 Some

 Most

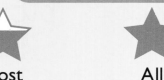 All

Letter shapes: r, n, h, b

1 Trace and write. Start at the green dot.

r r r

red   rain   rich

2 Trace and write. Start at the green dot.

n n n

nut   nail   neck

3 Trace and write. Start at the green dot.

h h h

hot   hand   help

Parent tip
Remember to ask your child to find and colour the monkey.

4 Trace and write. Start at the green dot.

b b b

Read and write.

Big bears blowing bubbles.

Letter shapes: m, k, p

5 Trace and write. Start at the green dot.

man   mud   milk

6 Trace and write. Start at the green dot.

kick   king   kiss

7 Trace and write. Start at the green dot.

pet   pop   play

8 Read and write.

Parrots playing the piano.

How much did you do?   Activities 1–8

Circle the star
to show what
you have done.

Some

Most

All

Letter shapes: c, a, o

1 Trace and write. Start at the green dot.

c   c   c

cat   cake   clock

2 Trace and write. Start at the green dot.

a   a   a

ant   axe   apple

Parent tip
Help your child to draw and cut out letters to make a name sign for their bedroom door.

3 Trace and write. Start at the green dot.

o   o   o

on   off   odd

4 Read and write.

Caterpillars crawling across cabbages.

Letter shapes: d, e, g

5 Trace and write. Start at the green dot.

duck · · day · · dig ·

6 Trace and write. Start at the green dot.

egg · eat · exit ·

7 Trace and write. Start at the green dot.

gap · game · girl ·

8 Read and write.

A dragon in a dress!

Letter shapes: q, f, s

1 Trace and write. Start at the green dot.

q q q

queen · quiz · quick

2 Trace and write. Start at the green dot.

f f f

fix · feet · frog

3 Trace and write. Start at the green dot.

s s s

sand · song · sleep

4 Read and write.

A queen queues quietly.

Parent tip
Practise joining the letter combination qu with your child to help with spelling.

Letter shapes: v, w, x, z

5 Trace and write. Start at the green dot.

V V V V

vet   van   visit

6 Trace and write. Start at the green dot.

W W W W

wall   web   wing

7 Trace and write. Start at the green dot.

X X X X

box   six   fox

8 Trace and write. Start at the green dot.

Z Z Z Z

zebra   zip   zoo

How much did you do?   Activities 1–8

Circle the star to show what you have done.

Some   Most   All

Rhyming words

Write the words from the top row next to the words they rhyme with. Then write down another word that rhymes. The first one has been done for you.

hug   hut   pan   fox   wish   ham

man   pan   ran

jug

jam

Parent tip
Suggest other words that rhyme with these and ask your child to write them out.

cut

fish

socks

Word endings: ff, ll, ss

2 Write the correct ending for each of these words.
Then write the whole word twice.

	ff	ll	ss

cli**ff**   cliff   cliff

she

dre

wa

o

we

sni

prince

stu

How much did you do?   ## Activities 1–2

Circle the star
to show what
you have done.

 Some    Most   All

15

Word endings: ck

1 Write ck at the end of each word. Then write out the whole word and join it to the correct picture.

Parent tip
Help your child to think of other words ending in ck and write them down.

ck

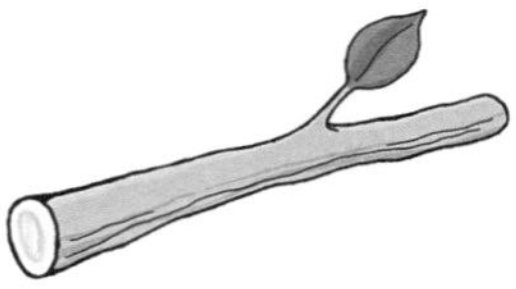

sock sock

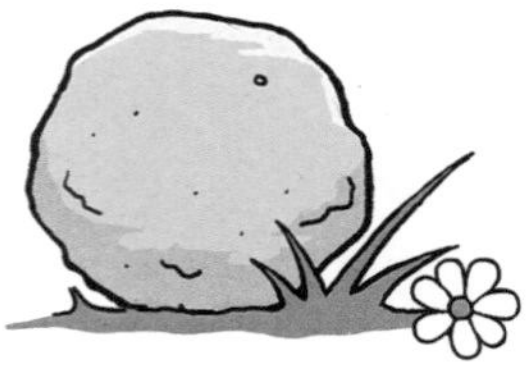

ki

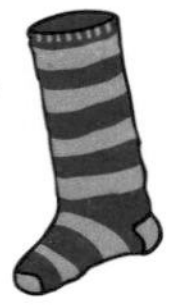

sti

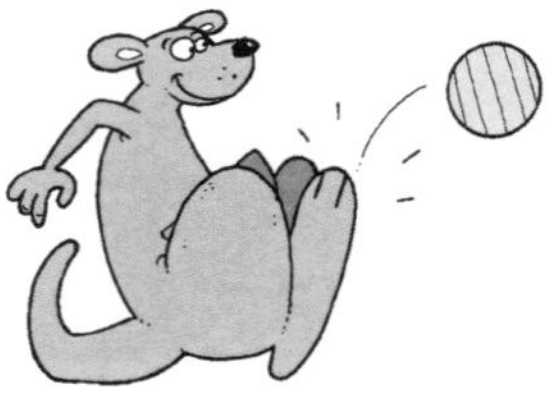

bri

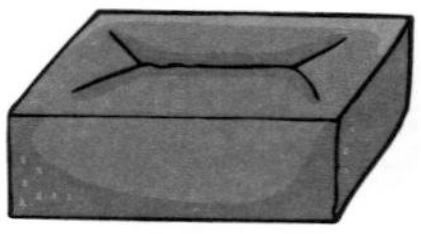

chi

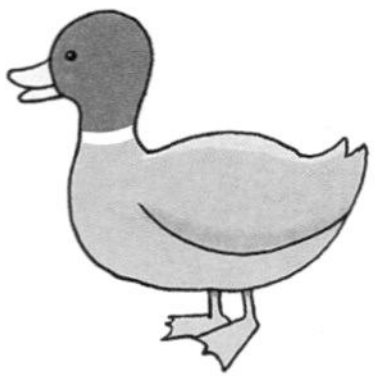

lo

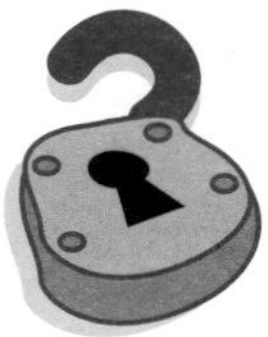

ro

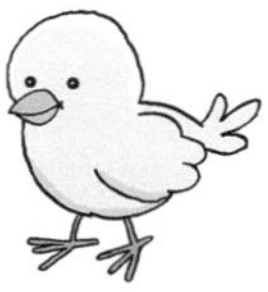

clo

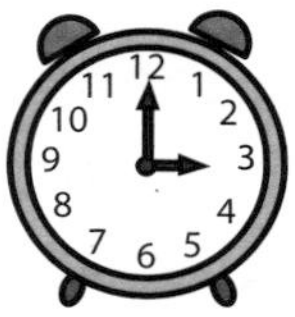

du

Word endings: ng

Write ng at the end of each word. Then write out the whole word and join it to the correct picture.

ng

strong   strong

ri

si

ki

swi

wi

stri

---

3 Read and write.

A sing-along song.

Vowel sounds: ai, ay

1 Trace and write. Start at the green dot.

snail   snail

afraid   afraid

play   play

delay   delay

train   train

away   away

2 Read and write.

The horses are eating hay again today.

Parent tip
Tilt the page slightly to help your child when tracing or writing sentences.

Days of the week

Trace and write. Start at the green dot.

Monday

Tuesday

Wednesday

Thursday

Friday

Saturday

Sunday

Monday
Tuesday
Wednesday
Thursday
Friday
Saturday
Sunday

How much did you do?   ## Activities 1–3

Circle the star
to show what
you have done.

Some

Most

All

Vowel sounds: ee, ea

1 Trace and write. Start at the green dot.

 bee *bee*

 tree *tree*

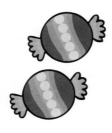 sweets *sweets*

 sheep *sheep*

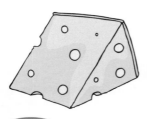 cheese *cheese*

Parent tip
Help your child practise letter joins like ee and ea in different words.

2 Trace and write. Start at the green dot.

 beach *beach*

 peas *peas*

 beads *beads*

 team *team*

3 Read and write.

The sheep take it easy.

Vowel sounds: ie, igh, y

1 Write words that rhyme next to the picture words below.
Some words match more than one picture.

try   tight   spy   tie   high   light

pie

fly

knight

Parent tip
Use the progress certificate at the back of this book to make a reward chart for your child.

2 Write these rhymes in your best handwriting. Then underline the igh spelling pattern in each line.

Star light, star bright,

First star I've seen tonight.

Wish I may, wish I might,

Have this wish I wish tonight.

Vowel sounds: oa, ow

1 Read the words with oa and ow below.

boat   toast   follow

boast   road   float

show   snow   know

tomorrow   toad   below

2 Write words with oa in them from the list above next to the boat.

float

Parent tip
Help your child make and decorate their own notebook for handwriting practice.

3 Look at the words at the top of page 24 again. Write words with ow in them next to the arrow.

show

4 Read and write.

A toad in a rowing boat.

_____

Vowel sounds: oo

1   Trace and write. Start at the green dot.

boot   boot

soon   soon

moon   moon

zoo   zoo

spoon   spoon

room   room

goose   goose

noon   noon

2   Read and write.

Owls hooting at the moon.

Parent tip
Think of more words with the vowel sound oo and write them for your child to copy.

Question words

We use these words to ask questions. Copy each word.

why who when what how where

Choose the correct word to begin each question below.
Then answer the question.

_____ is your birthday?

_____

_____ do you live?

_____

_____ often do you brush your teeth?

_____

_____ is your best friend?

_____

_____ is your favourite hobby?

_____

_____ is it important to eat fruit and vegetables?

_____

How much did you do?   ## Activities 1–4

Circle the star
to show what
you have done.

 Some   Most   All

27

Jokes

1 Read these jokes and copy them in your neatest handwriting.

Why did the sparrow fly into the library?

It was looking for bookworms.

Where do sick horses go?

To a horse-pital!

What's a cat's favourite colour?

Purrr-ple!

Parent tip
Help your child find more jokes from a book or the Internet to copy out.

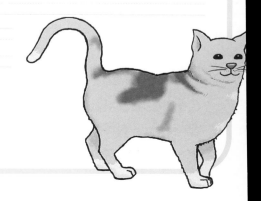

Copy this poem in your neatest handwriting.

I've got a dog as thin as a rail,

He's got fleas all over his tail.

Every time his tail goes flop,

The fleas on the bottom all hop to the top.

Circle the star
to show what
you have done.

Some

Most

All

Capital letters

1 Capital letters don't join to any other letters.
Trace and write. Start at the green dot.

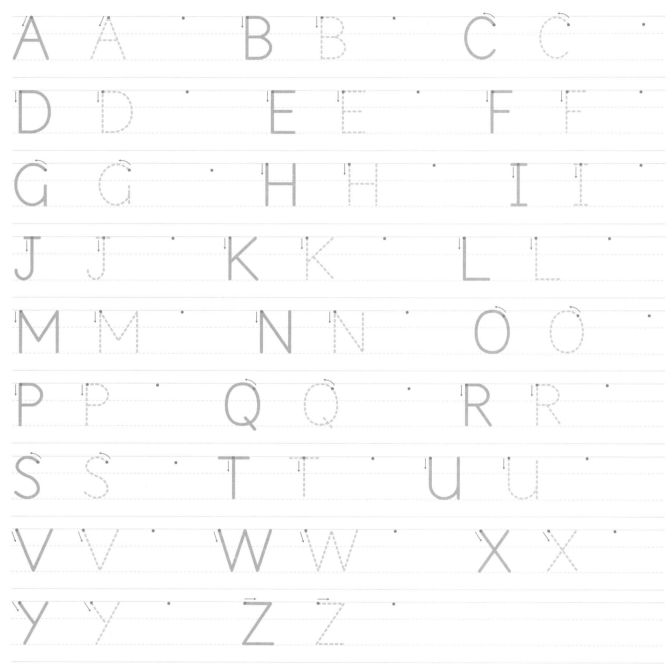

A A A   B B   C C

D D D   E E   F F

G G G   H H H   I I I

J J J   K K   L L L

M M M   N N N   O O

P P P   Q Q   R R

S S S   T T T   U U U

V V V   W W W   X X

Y Y Y   Z Z

Parent tip
Ask your child to write a list of their friends to practise capital letters.

30

You've got mail!

Write your name and address on the front of this envelope.
Begin each line with a capital letter.

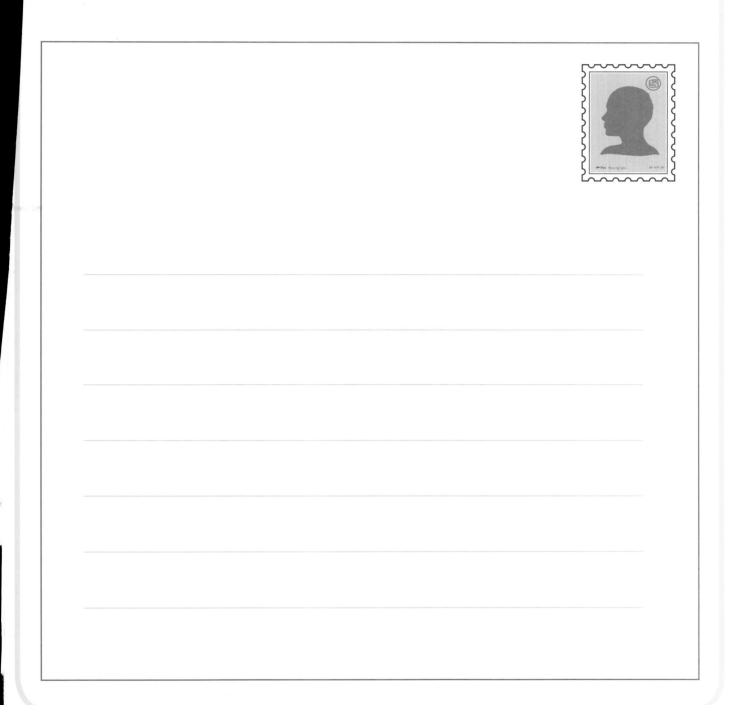

How much did you do?   Activities 1–2

Circle the star
to show what
you have done.

Some

Most

All

31

Check your progress

Did you find and colour all 15 monkeys?

(Including this one!)

- Shade in the stars on the progress certificate to show how much you did. Shade one star for every ⭐ you circled in this book.
- If you have shaded fewer than 10 stars go back to the pages where you circled Some or Most ⭐ and try those pages again.
- If you have shaded 10 or more stars you are ready to move on to the next workbook. Well done!

✂

Collins Easy Learning Handwriting Age 5–7 Workbook 2

Progress certificate

to

name _____

date _____

Count to ten Patterns	Letter shapes: l, t, i, u, y, j	Letter shapes: r, n, h, b, m, k, p	Letter shapes: c, a, o, d, e, g	Letter shapes: q, f, s, v, w, x, z	Rhyming words Word endings: ff, ll, ss	Word endings: ck, ng	Vowel sounds: ai, ay Days of the week	Vowel sounds: ee, ea	Vowel sounds: ie, igh, y	Vowel sounds: oa, ow	Vowel sounds: oo Question words	Jokes Hand-writing practice	Capital letters
pages 4–5	pages 6–7	pages 8–9	pages 10–11	pages 12–13	pages 14–15	pages 16–17	pages 18–19	pages 20–21	pages 22–23	pages 24–25	pages 26–27	pages 28–29	pages 30–31
⭐ 1	⭐ 2	⭐ 3	⭐ 4	⭐ 5	⭐ 6	⭐ 7	⭐ 8	⭐ 9	⭐ 10	⭐ 11	⭐ 12	⭐ 13	⭐ 14